# Love –

## when you lose the one you love...

by
Gwen Editin

*AuthorHouse™*
*1663 Liberty Drive, Suite 200*
*Bloomington, IN 47403*
*www.authorhouse.com*
*Phone: 1-800-839-8640*

*© 2007 Gwen Editin. All rights reserved.*

*No part of this book may be reproduced, stored in a retrieval system, or transmitted by any means without the written permission of the author.*

*First published by AuthorHouse 10/22/2007*

*ISBN: 978-1-4343-4103-7 (sc)*

*Printed in the United States of America*
*Bloomington, Indiana*

*This book is printed on acid-free paper.*

# L O V E

Love does not bring ownership
but only a feeling of belonging

of your heart having arrived and found
the right place to call "home" -

once in a lifetime
someone special enters your life

and a warmth lights your world
which will last, for as long as love lives

darkness and cold
no longer enemies

but things from the past
to remind you what is behind

understanding how
the heart needs to be warmed

the hand that holds the key
becomes what you long for

when your spirit is replenished
your faith rekindled

you learn how it is hope
that holds your dreams safe

and you find it is L O V E
that creates a life worth living.

# Dedicated

to my first husband
with whom I grew
and then grew apart

to my second husband
who was called Home

to my third husband
who challenges me

to a special friend
without whose patience and understanding
this book would have remained a dream.

# Table of Contents

## just as new dew   1
- until I dream   5
- for things we love   6
- if only   7
- when we were one   8
- the sound of echoes   9

## faith empowers hope   11
- the smile you brought   15
- when first we met   16
- was there something   17
- the things   18

## passion peaks only   19
- I close my eyes   23
- let me be sure   24
- I keep   25
- you   26
- you stole   27

## Love's imprint   29
- now all the love   33
- I know that   34
- if I knew   35
- how can I   36

## for things we love   37
- the whole   41
- if love   42
- would it be   43
- I feel the way   44

### as love returns  45
long after  49
you have always been  50
it's in my dreams  51
I knew that  52

### I will always feel  53
when words don't  57
I always thought  58
I should have  59
the colour of  60
the way I thought  61

### I need you to want  63
if you could only  67
I always knew  68
if one only knew  69
if I could  70

### passion...unites  71
I can't hold you  75
so many times  76
if it was meant  77
when it was time  78

### I looked for you  79
I have  83

### Ten Golden Rules for "Life After Loss"  87

Just as new dew awaiting the sun

Knows its transformation

brings not the end, but a new beginning ...

I hadn't told the children that your heart attack on Wednesday night while playing soccer, meant that Dad wouldn't be coming home - but I wrote down a few things, so we don't forget you.

Michael at age five, is the older brother to our daughter Kiera, age three. Kiera was still sleeping when Michael asked me when you're coming home.

I told him you had wanted to come home, but God wouldn't let you.

Michael said, "Mom, we should have taken more pictures of Daddy."

That was Friday, just before the funeral.

## until I dream

until I dream
I can't forget

the way love felt
the day you left

I miss the way
you held my hand

I miss the way
you smile and then

I can't explain
how two hearts know

they've said "goodbye"
but don't let go

without you here, your love remains
the only thing, I want to save

the same way that
I want you to

I know I'll feel
when you're gone too

the emptiness that fills me still
the loneliness that is my world

a thousand times
would I then keep

the dreams that you
made me believe.

## for things we love

for things we love
there will never be

time enough
for you and me

if I could hold you
instead of only

just a memory
of what you told me

the love I hold so deep inside
would always live
and never die

the moon stands still
when all I need

your lips on mine
for me to breathe

not knowing that you could not stay

I kept my promise
to love you always

the sun goes away
it never comes back

while I wait for you, I'll always feel that

which cannot be seen
but a prisoner be

captured by love
you brought to me.

## if only

if only, you had
let me do

the things for you
I wanted to

and if only, we had yesterday

I know just what
I should have said

the way that I
had thought that you

would find out that
you loved me too

for when we find that love still means
a place to live where hearts believe

and of those times
we shared so much

when all we felt
is how we loved

the way I know I'll always need

the things that you
have done for me

to teach my heart
how to forget

so it would know
before you left.

## when we were one

when we were one
then I became

someone who will never
be the same

all of my life
spent searching for

the one I knew
should come before

who makes me feel
who lets me love

those stolen moments
not enough

then it was time to give you back

to leave me lost
now only "half"

perhaps by now
I would have learned

to put things back
if you return

now I can't leave, the pain won't go

it follows me
so that I know

all of my life
spent loving "two"

now here I am
just wanting 'you'.

## the sound of echoes

the sound of echoes
heard by the heart

never so close
as when we're apart

I close my eyes
your image appears

I hear a voice
that brings you near

memory brings
your face to me

then I can't stop
what my heart sees

the promises made
no escape planned

the way I remember
you held my hand

my soul is still searching
for things that you brought

a reason to be
and then forget naught

to breathe in the way

your **s p i r i t** w a s

always to '**be**'

forever,

my **l o v e**.

faith empowers hope

to change love

from what was before.

The police came to take me to the hospital to identify your body, and I thought there may have been a mistake. When I saw you lying there, I could only touch your cheek, to let you know I had come as soon as I could.

I don't know why they kept repeating the details of the "incident" and why it was so important to mark the exact time of death, but it seemed forever before the police said "you can go now."

They told me I could take your shoes home, because they wouldn't need them.

## the smile you brought

the smile you brought
I never knew

meant only that
I'd love you too

more than what you thought you had

to give to me
to keep me, then

to see the sun
without you there

to feel a love, I cannot share

more than I want
and more than that

you brought me love
I can't forget

why can't you know
the things that I

feel that you should, if given time

the sound of echoes
heard by the heart

never so loud
as when we're apart

I breathe in the way
your spirit was

always to be,
forever, my love.

## when first we met

when first we met
I wanted you

to know how I
would want you too

but now I know
because you're gone

how love can feel when it belongs

to touch and feel
and taste the way

that love should be
when night is day

the moon lights up
the same way that

your eyes have said
you loved me and

you hold the key to all I've been

the other half
of who I am

the price for love
when it believes

it knows the things you are to me

new hope and meaning
to all that I've kept

the dreams, that my heart
will never forget.

## **was there something**

was there something else
I should have said

to let you know
I love you, and

if only, you had let me do

the things for you
I wanted to

that "something more"
you wanted that

I never gave
to you, and then

if only you had told me, that

you wanted to know
before you left

there's not a "next time"
when you were the first

to show me what
I had to learn

longing for that which I'll never have

searching for what
I already had.

## the things

the things you said
the way you smiled

the way I felt
was something I'll

never see, but only feel

the way that you
will always be

I knew some day
that I would love

I never thought you'd be the one

to change the way
that I believed

a heart should never
have that need

to show me what I waited for

was nothing like
I knew before

the way it feels
when I'm alone

that lets me know
it's found a home.

Passion peaks only

after it garners strength to begin again.

Kiera woke up crying for "Mommy". I went to comfort her and then tried to sleep. It seemed unfair that I was the one to have to tell others.

In the morning, I told Michael that your heart had stopped working and that you weren't coming home. Michael keeps asking why the doctor couldn't fix your heart. Just when I'm starting to forget, he asks me to tell him again how Daddy died.

Michael wanted to know if he could get another daddy, then he said "no, I want my own daddy back."

Then he smiled at me, looking for an answer.

Whenever Michael smiles, I see your smile again.

## I close my eyes

I close my eyes
to see you smile

I wait for you
to show me why

this heart of mine
will never be

the same as when
it never needed

I wait to see if maybe you

will find the words
I want you to

the ones I hope you mean to say

the way you looked
the other way

how can it be
so hard for you

to know that I will promise too

the way things are
when first you love

the love that makes
you want to touch

the heart that now says that it needs

to know if maybe
you'll love me.

## let me be sure

let me be sure
let my heart see

all of whatever
we were meant to be

the way that it was
and things that will never

be all that I thought - now gone forever

it cannot be
it will not laugh

it needs to find
what's gone, is past

when you were inside all of my soul

we were but one
both of us whole

I knew what I had
and it was enough

to know I could always
be sure of your love

it only needs to know why it is

that it needs to feel
in order to live

but how not to breathe
how not to know

if only it knew
how to let go.

## I keep

I keep the dream
of how things were

I hold the way
you always turned

the way you'd always be the one

that I would want
to hold and love

the way I need
for you to feel

that lets me know if you believe

in what could only
"be" if you

knew only then
all that I knew

then I would know
that you feel too

the way I need and want you to

all that you brought
I won't forget

I can't be more
than what you left

the way love is supposed to be

that when you love
you're never free.

## you

you taught me tears
and how to laugh

I want to know
how you did that

for who I am
all I can be

you taught me then
how I could see

to be myself, all that I am

the things that we
don't understand

I see your face
and long to touch

all that you are, that made me love

the way my heart
knows that it still

loves only you
and yet, until

it finds the place
that it should know

the place it used to call its home

now that you own
all that I was

before I knew
that it was love.

## you stole

you stole this heart
away from me

for now it knows
it cannot see

without your eyes
to see the sun

it needs for you
to be the one

who brings that peace
that comes with love

and all the ways two hearts can touch

you held my hand
and then you left

more memories, that
I won't forget

you brought me love not like before

when I was only
living for

the part of me
that you have found

belongs to you and only now

you make me want
to keep you close

to find the love
you made me know.

love's imprint leaves behind


certainty only


when it has found its way home.

We had decided to go to a summer resort this year and I had just mailed the deposit.

I asked Michael if we should all still go, and he wanted to know if you could still come fishing with us.

Michael keeps saying "Daddy, I love you" over and over. He wanted to know when he can see you again He cried just a little bit more and said he would be a good boy.

When I said, "If you close your eyes, you might be able to see Dad..." Michael quickly put on his pajamas to get ready for bed. He kissed his pillow and squeezed his eyes shut really tight, to make himself sleepy.

That night, I put money under his pillow with a note - "from Dad".

## now all the love

now all the love
I learned to hold

hugs me so tight
it won't let go

for all you said
and all you did

yesterday, today and looking ahead

keeping me close
to you once more

all that I knew
was that, before

the love you gave
that I had thought

some day, you'll know I've not forgot

there was a way
you made me feel

there was a time
when I could see

the way my heart
had stopped to hear

love pulled me through, when you were near

when love was mine
I knew I belonged

a place in your heart
is all that I want.

## I know that

I know that my heart
will always be

a prisoner of what
you made me feel

you didn't speak
but then you smiled

why can't you know
the things that I

will need to close my eyes to find

a dream I dreamt
when you were mine

you took my heart
my only friend

how could I know that it would end

without you here
I cannot feel

the nights we had
that were so real

the peace you brought
all that I need

the lonely nights now all I keep

not only now
but for all time

we shared a love
I'll never find.

## if I knew

if I knew I could love
the way I love you

then I would know
that "something more" too

to always be there
to hear one more thing

that you've said to me
that means "everything"

some hearts can be whole
when they live alone

but now, I know mine won't live on its own

you have my soul
and all of my heart

and what I've kept now
is only a part

the part left behind of all that we had

if I could have "more"
you would understand

to become "one" again
is all that I need

to be able to say that I had a dream

that came true at last
and, no matter when

I have to believe
I will see you again.

## how can I

how can I keep
the love that you left

what I know now
I will never forget

I know in my heart
when love remains

that this kind of love
just won't go away

how is it that, I can't forget

what I know now
is that it was meant

that I'll never love
the same way again

nothing could ever feel the same way

it's the way that I
want you to know

I hunger now
for something "more"

you brought more love
than one heart could hold

you gave me dreams that never grow old

and it feels like even
before I was born

it was always meant
that I would be yours.

for things we love


there is


never enough time.

The first thing next morning, Michael said "I love you so much, Daddy."

He looked up, just to see if you could hear him. I told him you could hear him, even if he just says it to himself.

So he said it again, a little bit louder – just in case.

I'm glad Michael says he feels you watching and following us everywhere. The Acura has only 1,394 km. on it. Before you died, I had never driven it. As we drove yesterday, Michael asked if we could open the sunroof, so you could see us better. When I opened the sunroof, Michael blew a kiss "to go way up high," he said.

Funny, I keep thinking of things I meant to tell you.

## the whole

the whole of my heart
that you took with you

was something that left
because it needs to

be closer to you
to feel alive

to understand "need" - is something that I

had always thought
that I'd grow "to be"

but not like how you
have made me feel

the love in your eyes
that lives in your heart

I want to keep
wherever you are

I always knew, that love could mean

I'd want for you
to never leave

but what I knew, was before you came

what I know now -
I won't love again

the same way that
I felt how you

would always be
my world of two.

## if love

if love has a way
to make you see

I will always love you
as long as I breathe

if "forever" were not
so short a while

I'd say I'd love you
for all that time

but if only I knew
which way I could be

closer to you to show I believe

the time that measures
how I love

is something more
than how you've touched

a heart that opens just for you

the things you say
and what you do

you smiled at me
to let me know

you're all I need
or want to hold

I want to know
how you knew that

you'd make me want
to love again.

## would it be

would it be wrong
to always want you

to be by my side
so that you too

can feel what I feel
to know how I love

the way that it feels, whenever we touch

can I be wrong
for wanting the sun

to always be there
when you are the one

who brings the light, who makes me feel

the only way love
can ever be real

you held my hand
and it was then

I knew that my life, would always be spent

waiting for you
to come back to me

I want you to have
all the love that I keep

I don't want to know
what love can be

until you're the one
to share all my dreams.

## I feel the way

I feel the way
my spirit soars

to meet some place
along with yours

the way you give
my soul 'that' peace

so that it knows what to believe

I never thought
the way I love

would mean some day
you'd be the one

to steal my heart
and hold the key

to what it is that love can be

I thank the Lord
that you were sent

to be my friend
the day we met

and now my heart
says it can't breathe

until you say that you believe

in love that's meant
for only two

the way that I
remember you.

as love returns


the heart still searching


reaffirms that it will never die.

Your daughter Kiera is precious, she is so young.

She told me she remembered you'd said you shouldn't lift Michael any more because it hurt your chest. She reminded me that when she was a baby she was light, but that Michael was too heavy. I told her that you had had the chest pains before you lifted them, and you had told me that you would have liked to hold them more.

Then I cried and she brought me a tissue. As she wiped my tears, she said, "Mommy, please don't cry, because when you cry – you make me cry too."

Her eyes got red, but she smiled bravely – so she wouldn't make me cry again.

How does one live without a heart?

## long after

long after my eyes
have lost sight of you

I know that my heart
has followed you to

wherever you are
whatever you do

I want to know
if maybe you knew

when you said goodbye
and waved your hand

I needed to know if maybe you had

the same dreams that I
have always kept

safe in my heart
to never forget

then I remember
you're always with me

not knowing that I would be keeping

all of the times
that we were so close

to hold in my heart
so then it's almost

the way that I thought
our love should be

and it was meant
I would never be free.

## you have always been

you have always been
the missing half

of who I am
and when I laugh

I know it's you
and what you've done

that brings me light
and not the sun

of all the love
that I once knew

how is it, that it's only you

who makes me 'want'
so that I need

the way I know
you make me feel

I live each day with hope that you

will find the love
I know that to

remember all
of what you gave

means only that
I'll love again

all my tomorrows
would be yesterday

if I'd only known
that you couldn't stay.

## it's in my dreams

it's in my dreams
that things are fine

and in that world
you're always mine

I keep the way
you looked at me

to be my guide so I can see

I feel the way
I know that when

you're close to me
the time we spent

that tells my heart
what it must feel

when we're apart
love's never real

it cannot be that you are gone

you took the part
I know belongs

within my heart
the way that I

know that it's you
but not know why.

## I knew that

I knew that before
when I loved only you

the way that I loved
I lived with hope to

be strong in a way
that I had learned

when you were here
and when all things were

the way that I'd dreamed
they'd always be

the things that I loved and I believed

when two hearts are joined
it's not meant to be

they grow far apart
so that they can't feel

the love that they shared to never grow old

but it was meant
their world should hold

all of the love
they always knew

when promises made
were meant for two

and hope that would echo
their love could be

all of whatever
it was meant to be.

I will always feel . . .

I will always care and


I will always love you.

Before you died, I had seen Michael whisper in your ear that he wanted ten stickers for his hockey album. I had shouted from upstairs, "I heard that, don't buy him any more stickers. I just bought him some yesterday."

I know Michael had whispered back, "Daddy, get me five instead."

Today, I told Michael, "When Daddy died, he told me to get you ten stickers." When I gave them to him, he was so pleased that you had had "the last word."

He didn't open them right away, but counted them out over and over – just to be sure there were ten.

I don't know why he did it so many times, he knows his numbers so well…

## when words don't

when words don't speak
and love remains

when all I feel
is just the same

before, my heart
knew what to say

how not to feel or be afraid

now all it needs
is someone who

brings all the love
that you brought too

if you come back
to me one day

I'd say the words I didn't say

the times we shared
I didn't know

would be the ones
I want to hold

within my heart
where you belong

all of this time, I was so wrong

to think that I
could still be whole

without the love
that now I know.

## I always thought

I always thought
that you would be

someone I loved
but not how I need

to know that you're safe - or if you can

tell me you miss
the things that we had

to hear what it is
that keeps calling me back

I wouldn't have said, I was sure that

I'd know what to say
if I saw you again

except that I feel
the love that you gave

as I keep searching, I can't seem to find

the things that you brought
that I thought were mine

I always was sure, how much I had loved

but never quite sure
the reasons for such

now I only remember
that you were the one

who made my life different
then taught me to love.

## I should have

I should have known
without you, life would be

none of the things
I wanted for me

I knew that, before
I had always believed

the love that we had
was something I'd keep

all of "forever" - but only if you

were waiting for me
to make all that true

I needed to say
before you had left

all of the ways, I'll never forget

how I would hold you
close to my heart

the things that I feel
when we're apart

the way that I know, I'll always need

the part of my soul
that chose to leave

the day that I said
I would see you again

I thought that you knew
I would always be waiting.

## the colour of

the colour of sorrow
would be the shade

of the love that I know
will not come again

so many times
I was never sure why

I thought that 'forever'
had meant you and I

would always remember when love was new

and never forget
how memories grew

the feelings that I've
never known from before

they remind me again
that I still want more

of the way that I felt when you were here

you told me tomorrow
would always be shared

wherever you've gone
I miss your smile

the things that we shared tell me that I'll

still be here waiting
for as long as it takes

to find your heart lives
so mine won't break.

## the way I thought

the way I thought
that love should be

only tomorrow
is what we need

which memories live
we don't always know

I only know mine
will never let go

but it's only now, that I can feel
the way I thought, our love would be

it's only now
that you've been here

that now I know
what I should fear

and it's only now
that I can see

the things I know
I must believe

in things unseen, in love untold
and all of what - two hearts can hold

and now if only
I could be sure

it's me, that you want
no longer 'her'.

I need you to want, and I want you to need . . .


the same way that I


want you for me.

I went through the wedding album with the children so they could remember you better. They are so young, I wouldn't want them to forget you too soon.

Michael asked me "When I grow up and get married – who is going to look after you, mom?"

Your friend had told me when you were playing soccer, you had stopped and said you felt dizzy. When you collapsed, you couldn't sit up although you had tried to.

You must have been trying to come back to us, but God wouldn't let you.

We had known about your heart disease for some time and I guess He had decided you had suffered enough.

## **if you could only**

if you could only understand
my heart belongs to you

it's then

that you would know
how much it means

to pay the price
for what I feel

two halves were meant
to be one whole

and when I sleep, it's then I know

that in my dreams
the love we had

is something
that I know I can

always hold, whenever I

remember you
and all the times

when you had meant
to tell me that

the love we shared
was something then

that you could feel the reason for

the love we had -
that was "before".

## I always knew

I always knew
that love should be

not only 'me'
but meant that "we"

would find the words
you cannot speak

the words I hear
are those I need

to know that you are feeling and
if somehow I could show you that

I always thought
that you would see

the same things that
I see for "we"

the things you meant
to say last time

perhaps you meant
to say you 're mine

I wanted you to know that I
had always thought - I'd have more time

to show you how
I wanted to be

all of the things
you were to me.

## if one only knew

if one only knew
that things will change

why loneliness wins
over love that remains

I thought today, that you should know

you brought more dreams
than one heart can hold

for "always", "forever"
and even beyond

that which I never, knew should belong

those times that I thought
I would never grow tired

of wanting to know
whenever you smiled

until you return
to lie here with me

all that I want, I only can dream

I live for the day
I will see you again

I wait for the time
no matter if, when

when all that I want, you took with you

the day
that you left

and my heart left too.

## if I could

if I could hold you
one more time

I might recall
the reasons why

that when it's right
it feels like home

the things that only
hearts could know

I was the one
who loved you more

if only then
you'd made it clear

that love sometimes, can fade away
and that you knew, you could not stay

I wanted something
more for me

but only if
your heart was free

through all the times that we had shared
I never knew how much I cared

until the day
you left me, and

I felt my heart -
alone, again.

Passion ... unites

but

love endures

forever.

I went to the bank to close your account, the one that had only $75.00 left in it.

Michael announces that "My Daddy died." No one knew how to respond exactly, but they said I would need to bring them a copy of the death certificate in order to "process your request."

There will be more financial decisions later, but your T4 also arrived. We had a bet as to whose earnings would be the most for last year. You were right.

You always said I never told you that you were right, often enough.

I also knew that you could never stay mad for long.

## I can't hold you

I can't hold you
any tighter

than the way
I want you now

I thought to keep you closer
but it seems to me, somehow

if you were ever
near to me

I'd never let
you go

and if I could
have held you more

my love for you
would show

you, all the ways that love can be
safe inside my world of dreams

the way I can't
forget your smile

the way I feel
whenever I

remember what you were to me
that no one else could ever be

the way you carried me, over the hill
so all that I want, is only you - still.

## so many times

so many times
you held my hand

so many ways, you loved me - that

I didn't want
to say goodbye

I hoped that you
would tell me I'll

never be alone the way

that now you're gone
I must remain

outside the world
you brought to me

the things we had -
I'd always believed

that you would remember
all that I feel

and you would know
it's in my dreams

that all my heart
says how it cares

the same way that I
now look for you here.

## if it was meant

if it was meant
that we should be

more than what
you are to me

then I would think
that maybe you

could love the way
I want you to

if I could only
see your face

I know I'll learn
to love again

without the fear and all the hope
and with your love, then I would know

how we could be
all that you want

and you would say
you never thought

the "all" I'd want
was just for you

to be the one
that I'd run to.

## when it was time

when it was time
to say goodbye

I thought that you
would tell me I'll

never be alone
the way

that now you're gone
I must remain

so many times
you held my hand

so many ways
you loved me and

inside the world
you built for me

I hold you close
and always feel

how sure I am, to wait for you
to come back, when it's your time to

tell me why
I only need

the dreams that you
had given to me.

I looked for you, the other day -

as far as the eye could see ...

but then I remembered, you were in my heart

and that, you'd always be.

I took the children to the cemetery. To let you know we came, we each put a footprint in the snow in front of your headstone.

Flowers had been left there by someone else. Michael kept peeking under them to see if you were really there. He said he wanted to check - that you were really dead.

Soon the children were off stamping footprints in the snow throughout the churchyard. Then it was time to leave.

We'll be back soon, but you know that.

## I have

I have loved you
from a distance

and I have loved you
from close up

and I know
I'll always love you

even though you may not love

the same way
that I always will

know that you're meant for me

the way I know
that you have been

the only one I need

I loved you when you couldn't talk
and say "those" things, but then

I hold forever in my heart
a love that has no end

so if you came
to tell me

that you thought
that you might stay

I'd take a chance
"tomorrow" 'd mean

much more
than just one day.

Once at home, I open the kitchen window and breathe in the promise of spring. Easter is approaching, the children keep asking if the Easter Bunny is still coming.

I say "of course." I'd like things to carry on, as normal.

In the meantime, I have decisions to make, documents to find, a new budget to plan.

I find out that the new car was not life insured. I hadn't been there when you bought it and we had joked that I had finally given you financial autonomy.

I'm glad that you had intended to be around to enjoy it. When I had told you we would grow old together, you had believed me.

# TEN GOLDEN RULES FOR "LIFE AFTER LOSS"

1. forgive your loved one, that they could not stay longer in this world
   - **spirits** may live forever, but bodies cannot

2. look for meaning in being the one who has been "left behind"
   - **remember** that we are never in control

3. acknowledge that no one can ever take their place
   - but that is, what was **meant** to be

4. grieve on each special occasion that your loved one is "missing"
   - be **comforted** that they still "hear" and "see" you

5. the greatest gift of love, is to carry on in place of your loved one
   - each day, do one thing in **honour** of their memory

6. allow yourself to treasure what is lost, to mourn what has happened
   - and to **grieve** what will never be...

7. feeling the pain of grief is a confirmation of your love
   - know that **love** lives on, for as long as you remember

8. rejoice for the one who has been "called home"
   - give them your blessing, that they may now **rest in peace**

9. **learn** from the past, do not regret it
   - promise yourself to look beyond for the "unopened" window


10. have **faith** that in time, you will find new love(s)
    - which will open your heart and heal your soul

**Live with hope and the dream of your spirits being re-united.**

## About the Author

The author currently
lives in Mississauga, Ontario
with her husband
and three children.

Recently receiving a diploma
from the
Institute of Children's Literature
completes a lifelong ambition
to pursue self-expression
that can make a difference.


Life is all about loving,
losing,
and then learning
to love again.

The author subscribes
to the theory
that life
is best lived
when choosing
that which we love –
hoping that somehow,
it will love us back.

## Her motto

"to think, before you speak

to feel,

before you write -

to know, before you love."

is free to everyone.

## About the Book

Throughout this book,
you are invited to go on a journey
which looks for answers
that lie within.

Our struggles teach us who we are.
Reading is one way
to learn from someone else's mistakes.

**Lesson #1:**

Leaving home at the age of 17
to live with your boyfriend
does not guarantee
that your first marriage will last forever.

**Lesson #2:**

When your second husband
dies of a heart attack
you find how life is mostly unpredictable.

**Lesson #3:**

A third marriage confirms
differences do not mean division.

**Lesson #4:**

No two loves are created equal
since they are determined
by the size of your heart.

Proceeds from this book to be donated to F.A.C.E.
Family Abuse Crisis Exchange – www.face1.org

Printed in the United States
95875LV00005B/181-288/A